# The Blooming Haven

*Unveiling the secrets of gardening for joy, Well-being, and Natural Abundance.*

By
Margharet J. Davis

© **Copyright 2023 by Margharet J.Davis - All rights reserved.**

The following Book is reproduced below with the goal of providing information that is as accurate and reliable as possible. Regardless, purchasing this Book can be seen as consent to the fact that both the publisher and the author of this book are in no way experts on the topics discussed within and that any recommendations or suggestions that are made herein are for entertainment purposes only. Professionals should be consulted as needed prior to undertaking any of the action endorsed herein.

This declaration is deemed fair and valid by both the American Bar Association and the Committee of Publishers Association and is legally binding throughout the United States.

Furthermore, the transmission, duplication, or reproduction of any of the following work including specific information will be considered an illegal act irrespective of if it is done electronically or in print. This extends to creating a secondary or tertiary copy of the work or a recorded copy and is only allowed with the express written consent from the Publisher. All additional right reserved.


The information in the following pages is broadly considered a truthful and accurate account of facts and as such, any inattention, use, or misuse of the information in question by the reader will render any resulting actions solely under their purview. There are no scenarios in which the publisher or the original author of this work can be in any fashion deemed liable for any hardship or damages that may befall them after undertaking information described herein.

Additionally, the information in the following pages is intended only for informational purposes and should thus be thought of as universal. As befitting its nature, it is presented without assurance regarding its prolonged validity or interim quality. Trademarks that are mentioned are done without written consent and can in no way be considered an endorsement from the trademark holder.

| | |
|---|---|
| Introduction | 6 |
| Chapter 1: Say It With Flowers | 9 |
| Chapter 3: It's Planting Time | 22 |
| Chapter 4: The Outdoor Garden | 29 |
| Chapter 5: Hedges and Trees | 38 |
| Chapter 6: The Vegetable Patch | 43 |
| Chapter 7: The Herb Garden | 49 |
| Chapter 8: Working in the Garden | 56 |
| Chapter 8: Getting Rid of Garden Pests | 62 |
| Chapter 9: Garden tools | 74 |
| Chapter 10: Healthy Gardening | 84 |
| Conclusion: | 90 |

# **Introduction**

Gardening is a timeless and universal practice that transcends cultural boundaries and connects people to the beauty and abundance of nature. It is an art form that allows individuals to cultivate and nurture plants, creating vibrant and serene spaces that bring joy and tranquility to both the gardener and those who behold the gardens.

In this introduction, we will embark on a journey into the fascinating world of gardening, exploring its rich history, its therapeutic benefits, and the endless possibilities it offers for self-expression, sustainability, and community engagement. Whether you have a sprawling backyard, a small balcony, or even just a few pots on a windowsill, gardening allows you to forge a deep connection with the natural world and discover the profound satisfaction of watching life bloom and thrive under your care.

At its core, gardening is a harmonious partnership with nature. It is about understanding the needs of plants and working in sync with the seasons, the soil, and the elements to create optimal conditions for growth. Through thoughtful planning, diligent nurturing, and continuous learning, gardeners cultivate not only plants but also a profound sense of connection with the earth and a reverence for the intricate web of life.

Gardening offers numerous physical, mental, and emotional benefits. It provides an opportunity to engage in physical activity, fostering strength, endurance, and flexibility. The act of tending to plants and witnessing their growth promotes mindfulness, reduces stress, and enhances overall well-being. Gardens also serve as sanctuaries, offering a respite from the fast-paced world and providing a space for reflection, relaxation, and rejuvenation.

Moreover, gardening is a sustainable practice that allows us to tread lightly on the earth and make a positive impact on the environment. By embracing organic gardening methods, conserving water, composting, and attracting beneficial insects, we create biodiverse ecosystems that support pollinators and other wildlife while minimizing our ecological footprint.

Throughout this exploration of gardening, we will delve into various topics such as soil health, plant selection and care, pest management, sustainable practices, and the therapeutic benefits of gardening. We will learn about the importance of creating a thriving ecosystem in our gardens, where plants, insects, birds, and other organisms coexist harmoniously, supporting each other's existence.

From the basics of digging in the soil and sowing seeds to the art of designing and creating beautiful landscapes, gardening offers endless opportunities for creativity and self-expression. It allows us to experiment with colors, textures, and scents, creating living works of art that delight the senses and inspire awe in all who experience them. Whether you have a passion for growing vibrant flowers, cultivating delicious vegetables, or creating serene and meditative spaces, gardening is a canvas for your imagination.

Whether you are a seasoned gardener or just beginning your green journey, this exploration of gardening will provide you with valuable insights, practical tips, and inspiration to cultivate your own piece of paradise. So grab your gardening gloves, prepare your tools, and join us as we embark on this rewarding and transformative adventure into the world of gardening. Together, let's nurture nature, create beauty, and reap the bountiful rewards of the garden.

# Chapter 1: Say It With Flowers

Introduction:

Flowers have a universal language that transcends barriers and speaks to our emotions. Throughout history, humans have used flowers as a means of communication, conveying sentiments and messages without words. This chapter explores the power and significance of flowers as a language of their own. From the symbolism of different flowers to the art of floral arrangements, we delve into how flowers can express love, gratitude, sympathy, celebration, and more. Whether it's a single bloom or an elaborate bouquet, saying it with flowers adds beauty, depth, and a touch of magic to our lives.

Paragraph 1: The Language of Flowers

Flowers have long been associated with symbolic meanings, allowing people to express emotions and messages in a subtle and elegant way. The language of flowers, also known as floriography, dates back centuries and was particularly popular during the Victorian era. Each flower carries its own significance and can convey a range of emotions. For example, roses are commonly associated with love and passion, while lilies symbolize purity and innocence. Sunflowers represent adoration and happiness, while daisies convey innocence and purity. Understanding the meanings behind different flowers allows us to choose the perfect bloom to express our sentiments.

## Paragraph 2: Love and Romance

When it comes to matters of the heart, flowers have a unique ability to convey love and romance. A bouquet of red roses is the classic symbol of passionate love, while pink roses represent admiration and sweetness. Other flowers, such as tulips, orchids, and daisies, also carry messages of love and affection. The way flowers are arranged can further enhance their romantic impact. A single long-stemmed rose can be a powerful declaration of love, while a lavish arrangement of mixed flowers can express a deep and abiding affection. Whether it's a bouquet given on Valentine's Day, an anniversary, or just to express your feelings, flowers have a way of speaking the language of love.

Paragraph 3: Gratitude and Appreciation

Flowers are a beautiful way to express gratitude and appreciation. Whether it's a simple bouquet of daisies or a bouquet of colorful gerbera daisies, these cheerful blooms convey a sense of appreciation and thankfulness. Sunflowers, with their vibrant yellow petals, symbolize adoration and gratitude. Additionally, mixed bouquets featuring a variety of flowers can capture the essence of appreciation and gratitude, allowing you to say thank you in a heartfelt and meaningful way. Whether it's expressing gratitude to a friend, a colleague, or a loved one, flowers are a wonderful way to show your appreciation.

Paragraph 4: Sympathy and Condolences

During times of loss and grief, flowers play an important role in expressing condolences and offering comfort. White lilies are often associated with funerals and represent purity and the renewal of the soul. Chrysanthemums, particularly in white or light colors, symbolize sympathy and honor. Roses in soft shades of pink or white can also convey messages of sympathy and support. Floral arrangements with delicate and soothing colors provide solace and show support to those who are grieving. Whether it's a wreath, a standing spray, or a floral arrangement sent to a funeral service, flowers can provide a meaningful expression of sympathy.

Paragraph 5: Celebration and Joy

Flowers are not limited to somber occasions; they also bring joy and celebration into our lives. Bright and colorful blooms, such as daffodils, tulips, and peonies, symbolize happiness, joy, and new beginnings. Gerbera daisies, with their bold and vibrant petals, are perfect for celebrating achievements and milestones. Floral arrangements that feature a mix of lively flowers can add a festive and cheerful ambiance to birthdays, anniversaries, and other joyful occasions. The vibrant colors and fragrant blooms of flowers have the power to uplift spirits and create a sense of happiness and excitement. Whether it's a grand floral centerpiece at a wedding reception or a simple bouquet gifted to celebrate a promotion, flowers have the ability to enhance the joyous atmosphere of any celebration.


Flowers also have the remarkable ability to convey specific messages and sentiments based on their colors. For instance, red flowers symbolize passion and deep affection, while yellow flowers represent friendship and happiness. Blue flowers are associated with tranquility and serenity, while purple flowers signify admiration and royalty. By selecting flowers with specific colors, you can tailor your message and enhance the overall impact of your floral gift.


Furthermore, the art of floral arrangement plays a crucial role in expressing emotions through flowers. The way flowers are arranged can create different moods and convey various meanings. A loose and wild arrangement exudes a sense of natural beauty and freedom, while a tightly clustered arrangement conveys elegance and formality. The choice of complementary or contrasting colors can evoke different emotions, such as harmony, excitement, or calmness. Each arrangement becomes a unique expression of the sender's intentions and emotions.

In addition to their symbolic meanings and visual appeal, flowers offer numerous psychological benefits. Studies have shown that being surrounded by flowers can elevate mood, reduce stress, and improve overall well-being. The presence of flowers in indoor spaces promotes a sense of relaxation and increases feelings of happiness and contentment. They have the power to brighten up a room and create a welcoming and positive environment. Incorporating flowers into your living or workspaces can significantly enhance the overall atmosphere and contribute to a more uplifting and harmonious ambiance.

In conclusion, saying it with flowers is a powerful and timeless way to communicate emotions and messages. From the language of flowers to the art of floral arrangement, flowers provide a means of expression that transcends language barriers and touches the heart. Whether it's conveying love, gratitude, sympathy, or celebrating joyous occasions, flowers have the ability to capture the essence of our sentiments and make a lasting impact. So, the next time you want to convey your emotions or add a touch of beauty to a special moment, let the language of flowers be your guide. Embrace the enchantment and magic of flowers and let their vibrant colors and fragrant blooms speak the words that sometimes cannot be expressed. Say it with flowers, and watch as their beauty and symbolism create lasting memories and cherished moments.

## Chapter 2: Houseplant Care & Maintenance

Introduction:
Houseplants have become an integral part of our indoor spaces, bringing a touch of nature and tranquility to our homes, offices, and other living environments. Caring for houseplants goes beyond mere decoration; it involves understanding their specific needs and providing the right conditions for their growth and well-being. In this chapter, we will explore the art of houseplant care and maintenance, covering various aspects such as watering, light requirements, fertilization, pest control, grooming, pruning, propagation, and the psychological benefits of living with plants. By delving into these topics, you will gain the knowledge and skills necessary to create thriving and thriving indoor gardens that enrich your surroundings and positively impact your well-being.

## Paragraph 1: Watering and Moisture

Watering is one of the fundamental aspects of houseplant care. Understanding the watering needs of different plant species is crucial for their health and vitality. Factors such as the type of plant, its size, the type of potting mix, humidity levels, and environmental conditions all contribute to determining the watering frequency and amount. It is important to strike a balance between underwatering and overwatering. Underwatering can lead to wilting and dehydration, while overwatering can suffocate the roots and cause root rot. The key is to provide sufficient water to keep the soil moist but not waterlogged. Regularly monitor the moisture level of the soil and adjust your watering schedule accordingly.

Paragraph 2: Light Requirements

Light is an essential factor for plant growth and development. Different houseplants have varying light requirements, ranging from low light to bright, direct sunlight. Understanding the light preferences of your plants is crucial to ensure their optimal growth. Low-light plants, such as snake plants and ZZ plants, can thrive in areas with minimal natural light. They are suitable for rooms with north-facing windows or areas away from direct sunlight. Medium-light plants, like pothos and philodendrons, prefer bright, indirect light and can tolerate some periods of direct sunlight. Bright-light plants, such as succulents and cacti, require several hours of direct sunlight each day. Placing your plants in locations that match their light requirements will help them thrive and avoid issues such as leggy growth or leaf burning.

Paragraph 3: Fertilization and Nutrients

To ensure the long-term health and vitality of houseplants, providing them with essential nutrients is crucial. While potting soil contains some nutrients, they eventually become depleted over time. Fertilizers supplement the nutrient requirements of plants, promoting healthy growth and vibrant foliage. Choose a balanced, water-soluble fertilizer specifically formulated for houseplants and follow the recommended dosage and frequency. During the active growing season, typically spring and summer, plants have higher nutrient demands and will benefit from regular fertilization. However, it is important not to overfertilize, as this can lead to nutrient imbalances and burn the roots. Always water your plants before applying fertilizer and flush the soil periodically to remove any salt buildup.

Paragraph 4: Pest Control

Pests can be a persistent challenge when it comes to houseplant care. Common pests that can infest indoor plants include aphids, mealybugs, spider mites, scale insects, and fungus gnats. Regular monitoring and early detection are crucial for effective pest control. Inspect your plants regularly, checking the leaves, stems, and soil for any signs of pest activity, such as sticky residue, webbing, or tiny crawling insects. If you spot pests, take immediate action to prevent further damage. Depending on the severity of the infestation, treatment options include using insecticidal soaps, neem oil, or introducing beneficial insects that prey on pests. Isolate infested plants to prevent the pests from spreading to other plants. Maintaining good plant hygiene by regularly cleaning the leaves, removing fallen debris, and ensuring proper airflow can help prevent pest infestations. Additionally, creating a healthy and balanced growing environment by providing adequate light, proper watering, and appropriate fertilization strengthens plants' natural defenses against pests.

Paragraph 5: Grooming, Pruning, and Propagation

Grooming and pruning are essential practices in houseplant care to maintain their appearance and promote healthy growth. Grooming involves removing dead or yellowed leaves, cleaning dust off the leaves, and occasionally wiping them with a damp cloth to enhance their beauty and ensure optimal photosynthesis. Pruning, on the other hand, focuses on shaping and controlling the growth of the plant. Regular pruning helps maintain the plant's desired form, prevents overcrowding, and encourages bushier growth. Trim leggy stems to promote branching and pinch back the tips of certain plants to promote fuller growth. Remember to use clean and sharp pruning tools to avoid causing damage or introducing infections.

Propagation is an exciting aspect of houseplant care that allows you to expand your collection and share the joy of plants with others. There are various methods of propagation, including stem cuttings, leaf cuttings, division, and offshoots. Each method requires specific techniques and conditions, but they generally involve selecting healthy plant parts, preparing them for rooting, and providing the right environment for the development of new roots. Propagation can be a rewarding process that allows you to witness the growth and development of new plants, fostering a deeper connection with your houseplants.

Conclusion:

Houseplant care and maintenance require a combination of knowledge, observation, and nurturing. By understanding the specific needs of your houseplants and implementing proper care techniques such as watering, providing adequate light, fertilizing appropriately, controlling pests, grooming, pruning, and propagation, you can create a thriving and vibrant indoor garden. The rewards of caring for houseplants extend beyond their visual appeal, as they contribute to improved air quality, reduced stress levels, and a sense of well-being. Embrace the journey of cultivating a green oasis within your home, and enjoy the beauty, serenity, and connection with nature that houseplants bring. Remember, with patience, attention, and a little love, your houseplants will flourish and bring joy to your living space for years to come.

# **Chapter 3: It's Planting Time**

Introduction:

The arrival of spring brings with it the promise of new beginnings and the excitement of planting. As the days grow longer and the temperatures rise, gardeners and plant enthusiasts eagerly prepare their tools and gather their seeds, ready to embark on a journey of growth and transformation. In this chapter, we will explore the beauty and importance of planting, from the joy of sowing seeds to the satisfaction of watching plants thrive. Join us as we delve into the art and science of planting and discover the wonders that await in the soil.

## Paragraph 1: The Magic of Seeds

Seeds are the embodiment of potential.

They hold within them the blueprint of life, waiting for the right conditions to sprout and grow. As gardeners, we become custodians of this magic, carefully selecting seeds that align with our vision. The act of planting a tiny seed is a gesture of hope and faith in the cycles of nature. Whether it's a packet of vegetable seeds destined to become a bountiful harvest or a collection of flower seeds that will transform a patch of land into a vibrant tapestry of colors, sowing seeds is where the journey begins.

Seeds come in many shapes, sizes, and forms. Some are small and delicate, like the tiny specks of basil or lettuce, while others are larger and more robust, like the kernels of corn or sunflower. Each seed carries within it the potential for growth, waiting for the right combination of moisture, warmth, and nutrients to awaken its dormant life force. It is a marvel to witness the transformation of a tiny seed into a flourishing plant, bearing leaves, flowers, and fruits.

## Paragraph 2: Preparing the Ground

Successful planting starts with preparing the ground. This involves clearing away debris, loosening the soil, and improving its structure and fertility. Begin by removing any weeds or rocks that may hinder plant growth. Use a garden fork or tiller to break up compacted soil, allowing roots to penetrate and access essential nutrients. Incorporating organic matter, such as compost or well-rotted manure, enriches the soil, promotes beneficial microbial activity, and improves water retention. By investing time and effort in preparing the ground, we create a nurturing environment for our plants to thrive.

The process of preparing the ground is a mindful and meditative practice. It connects us to the earth and reminds us of our role as caretakers of the land. As we clear away debris, we release the past and make way for new growth. As we till the soil, we break up stagnation and create space for roots to explore and absorb nutrients. And as we enrich the soil with organic matter, we replenish its vitality and create a foundation for abundant growth.

Paragraph 3: Choosing the Right Plants

The choices we make when selecting plants can determine the success of our garden. Factors such as climate, sunlight exposure, and soil conditions play a crucial role in determining which plants will thrive in a specific location. Consider the unique characteristics of your garden and choose plants that are well-suited to those conditions. Whether you prefer the vibrant petals of annual flowers, the lush foliage of perennials, or the practicality of growing your own vegetables and herbs, selecting the right plants ensures a harmonious and fruitful garden.

When choosing plants, it's important to consider their specific needs and requirements. Some plants thrive in full sun, while others prefer partial shade. Some require well-draining soil, while others can tolerate wetter conditions. By understanding the needs of different plants, we can create microenvironments within our garden that cater to their individual preferences. This not only ensures the health and vitality of the plants but also enhances the overall aesthetics and functionality of the garden.

Paragraph 4: Planting Techniques and Care

Planting techniques vary depending on the type of plant, but there are general principles to follow. Prepare holes or furrows at the appropriate depth and spacing, following the instructions provided with seeds or seedlings. Gently place the seeds or transplants in their designated spots, cover them with soil, and gently press down to ensure good seed-to-soil contact. Water the newly planted area thoroughly to settle the soil and provide initial moisture. As the plants grow, provide proper care, including regular watering, mulching to retain moisture and suppress weeds, and feeding with organic fertilizers. Regular observation and pest management are also essential to ensure healthy growth.

Watering is a critical aspect of plant care, especially during the early stages of growth. New plants have delicate root systems that require consistent moisture to establish themselves in the soil. The frequency and amount of water needed vary depending on factors such as plant type, weather conditions, and soil composition. It's important to strike a balance and avoid overwatering, which can lead to root rot, or underwatering, which can stunt growth and cause wilting.

Mulching is another valuable practice in plant care. Applying a layer of organic mulch around plants helps retain moisture in the soil, regulate temperature, suppress weed growth, and enhance overall soil health. Organic materials such as wood chips, straw, or shredded leaves make excellent mulch options. Apply a layer of mulch around plants, ensuring it doesn't touch the stems directly to prevent rotting.

Feeding plants with organic fertilizers is crucial for providing essential nutrients. These fertilizers nourish the soil and promote healthy growth without the risk of chemical imbalances. Organic options include compost, well-rotted manure, and organic plant-based fertilizers. Follow the recommended application rates and timing based on the specific needs of the plants. Regular feeding helps sustain vigorous growth, enhances flowering and fruiting, and builds resilience against pests and diseases.

Regular observation is key to maintaining plant health. Keep an eye out for any signs of stress, such as wilting, discoloration, or pest infestations. Early detection allows for prompt intervention, preventing further damage and ensuring the plants' well-being. Establish a routine of inspecting your garden, checking leaves, stems, and flowers for any abnormalities. Familiarize yourself with common pests and diseases that affect your chosen plants, so you can take appropriate measures to mitigate their impact.

Paragraph 5: Cultivating a Lasting Relationship

Planting goes beyond the act of sowing seeds and nurturing young plants. It is a relationship that evolves over time, as we tend to the needs of our growing garden. It is a dance between the gardener and the soil, a constant dialogue between humans and nature. We learn to read the signs, adapting our care to the changing seasons and the unique requirements of each plant. We celebrate the first signs of growth, eagerly anticipate the emergence of flowers and fruits, and find solace in the peacefulness of tending to our garden. The act of planting is an invitation to connect with the natural world, to become attuned to its rhythms, and to cultivate a lasting relationship with the land.

A successful garden is not only a result of diligent care and attention but also a testament to our ability to coexist with nature harmoniously. By practicing sustainable gardening methods, such as conserving water, using organic fertilizers, and minimizing chemical interventions, we contribute to the health of our environment. We invite beneficial insects, birds, and other wildlife into our garden, creating a balanced ecosystem that thrives in symbiosis. As we cultivate a lasting relationship with the land, we deepen our connection to the earth and gain a profound appreciation for the interconnectedness of all living things.

Conclusion:

In conclusion, planting time is a season of possibilities, growth, and connection. It is a time to immerse ourselves in the beauty of nature, to nurture life, and to cultivate a deep sense of fulfillment. Through the act of planting, we embark on a journey of discovery, learning from the wisdom of nature and finding solace in its rhythms. So, let us embrace the magic of planting, as we sow the seeds of beauty, nurture the soil, and create thriving gardens that are a testament to our love for the natural world.

# **Chapter 4: The Outdoor Garden**

Introduction:

The outdoor garden is a sanctuary of nature's beauty, a place where we can escape the confines of indoor spaces and immerse ourselves in the wonders of the natural world. It is a haven of tranquility, a canvas for creativity, and a source of inspiration. In this chapter, we will explore the magic and joys of the outdoor garden, from designing and planning to the cultivation of plants and the creation of inviting spaces. Join us as we delve into the elements that make the outdoor garden a place of endless possibilities.

Paragraph 1: Designing Your Garden

Designing an outdoor garden is akin to creating a work of art. It requires careful thought, consideration of space, and an understanding of the elements that make a garden visually appealing and functional. Start by envisioning the overall style or theme you desire, whether it's a formal garden with structured lines and symmetrical features, a cottage garden bursting with colors and textures, or a minimalist garden focused on simplicity and harmony. Consider the size and shape of your garden, as well as the surrounding landscape and architecture, to ensure a cohesive design that integrates seamlessly with its surroundings.

Within the overall design, consider the layout of different garden areas, such as flower beds, pathways, seating areas, and focal points. Pay attention to the flow of movement, creating paths that invite exploration and areas that encourage relaxation and contemplation. Incorporate elements of interest, such as water features, sculptures, or arbors, to add visual appeal and create focal points. By carefully designing your outdoor garden, you can create a space that reflects your personal style and provides a delightful experience for both visitors and yourself.

Paragraph 2: Selecting Plants for Your Garden

Choosing the right plants is crucial to the success of your outdoor garden. Consider the climate and environmental conditions of your region, such as sunlight exposure, temperature range, and soil type, to select plants that are well-suited to thrive in those conditions. Research different plant species and varieties, taking into account their growth habits, maintenance requirements, and compatibility with other plants. Aim for a diverse selection of plants that provide year-round interest, with a mix of flowering plants, foliage plants, and evergreens.

When selecting plants, think about their various characteristics, such as color, texture, height, and bloom time. Create a harmonious palette of colors by choosing plants with complementary or contrasting hues. Consider the texture of leaves and flowers, combining fine-textured plants with bold or coarse-textured ones for visual interest. Vary the heights of plants to create depth and dimension in your garden, with taller plants at the back or center and shorter ones at the front or edges. By carefully curating your plant selection, you can create a garden that is visually captivating and offers a diverse range of sensory experiences.

Paragraph 3: Creating Functional Spaces

A well-designed outdoor garden goes beyond aesthetics and incorporates functional spaces that enhance the overall enjoyment of the garden. Consider the activities you envision in your garden, whether it's hosting gatherings, dining al fresco, practicing yoga, or simply finding a quiet spot to read a book. Allocate areas for these activities, creating dedicated spaces with appropriate seating, tables, or amenities. Integrate shade structures, such as pergolas or umbrellas, to provide relief from the sun, and incorporate lighting to extend the usability of the garden into the evening hours.

Additionally, think about the importance of pathways and circulation within the garden. Create clear pathways that guide visitors through different areas, providing an intuitive and pleasant journey. Use materials such as gravel, stone, or pavers to define pathways and add texture. Ensure pathways are wide enough to accommodate comfortable movement and consider incorporating curves or meandering paths to add intrigue and a sense of discovery. By thoughtfully designing functional spaces, you create a garden that not only looks beautiful but also serves as a practical and inviting outdoor living space.

Paragraph 4: Nurturing Your Plants

Once you've designed and planted your outdoor garden, it's essential to provide proper care and maintenance to ensure the health and vitality of your plants. Regular watering is crucial, especially during dry spells or hot weather, to keep the soil moist and prevent dehydration. Be mindful of the specific water needs of each plant, as some may require more frequent watering than others. Mulching around plants helps conserve moisture, suppress weeds, and regulate soil temperature. Apply a layer of organic mulch, such as wood chips or straw, around the base of your plants, taking care not to pile it directly against the stems.

Fertilizing your plants is another vital aspect of their care. Choose a balanced organic fertilizer and apply it according to the recommended dosage and frequency. This will provide essential nutrients that promote healthy growth and abundant blooms. Regularly inspect your plants for signs of pests or diseases, such as yellowing leaves, wilting, or spots. Early detection allows for prompt intervention, whether it's through organic pest control methods or appropriate disease management strategies. Prune and trim your plants as needed to maintain their shape, remove dead or damaged parts, and encourage new growth.

Paragraph 5: Seasonal Care and Maintenance

The outdoor garden requires ongoing care throughout the seasons to adapt to changing conditions and ensure its longevity. In spring, prepare your garden for the growing season by clearing debris, loosening the soil, and applying a layer of compost or organic matter to enrich the soil. This is also the time to sow seeds or plant seedlings for annuals and vegetables. During summer, be vigilant about watering, particularly during heatwaves, and provide shade for sensitive plants. Deadhead spent flowers to encourage continuous blooming and remove weeds regularly to prevent competition for nutrients.

In autumn, prepare your garden for the cooler months ahead by removing spent annuals, cutting back perennials, and clearing fallen leaves. Apply a layer of mulch to protect plant roots from freezing temperatures and conserve moisture. It's also an excellent time for planting bulbs for spring blooms. Winter care involves protecting sensitive plants from frost or freezing temperatures by covering them with blankets or frost cloth. Continue monitoring for pests and diseases, as certain issues may persist even in colder months. Use this time to plan and prepare for the upcoming gardening season by researching new plant varieties or redesigning garden areas.

Paragraph 6: Encouraging Wildlife and Biodiversity

An outdoor garden is not just a space for plants; it's also an opportunity to create a thriving ecosystem that supports biodiversity. Encourage beneficial insects, birds, and other wildlife to visit your garden by providing food sources, such as nectar-rich flowers or bird feeders. Incorporate plants that attract pollinators, such as bees and butterflies, to promote healthy plant reproduction. Create habitats, such as birdhouses or insect hotels, to offer shelter and nesting sites.

Avoid using harmful pesticides or chemicals that can disrupt the delicate balance of the ecosystem. Instead, practice natural pest control methods, such as companion planting or introducing beneficial insects like ladybugs or praying mantises. By creating a welcoming environment for wildlife, you contribute to the overall health of your garden and the surrounding environment.

Paragraph 7: Garden Maintenance and Organization

Keeping your outdoor garden tidy and well-organized not only enhances its visual appeal but also makes it easier to care for and enjoy. Regularly remove weeds to prevent them from competing with your plants for nutrients and water. Use appropriate tools, such as a hoe or hand trowel, to carefully extract weeds without disturbing the surrounding plants. Prune your plants as needed to maintain their shape and prevent overcrowding. Properly dispose of any plant debris to maintain a clean and healthy garden environment.

Consider implementing an organization system for your garden tools and supplies. Having a designated area for storing tools, such as a shed or tool rack, ensures that they are easily accessible and protected from the elements. Use labeled containers or shelves to store seeds, fertilizers, and other gardening essentials, keeping them organized and readily available when needed.

Regularly inspect and maintain your garden structures, such as trellises, arbors, or raised beds. Repair any damage or instability to ensure the safety and longevity of these elements. Clean and maintain pathways and seating areas by removing debris, pressure washing surfaces if necessary, and repairing any unevenness or cracks.

In addition to physical maintenance, it's essential to regularly reassess and adapt your garden to your evolving preferences and needs. Evaluate the success of different plantings and make note of any areas that require improvement or adjustment. Consider experimenting with new plant varieties or introducing different design elements to keep your garden fresh and exciting. Gardening is an ongoing journey of learning and growth, and your garden should reflect your evolving tastes and desires.

Paragraph 8: Enjoying the Fruits of Your Labor

Finally, the outdoor garden is a space meant to be enjoyed and savored. Take time to relax and soak in the beauty and serenity of your garden. Create inviting seating areas where you can unwind, read a book, or simply bask in the natural surroundings. Host gatherings and share the beauty of your garden with friends and loved ones, creating lasting memories in this enchanting outdoor oasis.

Harvest the fruits, vegetables, and herbs you've cultivated with care. Celebrate the bounty of your garden by incorporating the fresh produce into your meals, sharing with neighbors, or preserving for later use. Take pride in the flowers you've nurtured and create stunning floral arrangements to brighten your home or gift to others.

Remember to be present in your garden and observe the small miracles that unfold each day. Notice the delicate unfurling of a new leaf, the dance of a butterfly among the flowers, or the soothing sound of a gentle breeze rustling the leaves. Embrace the connection with nature that your outdoor garden provides and find solace and inspiration in its ever-changing beauty.

Conclusion:

The outdoor garden is a place of endless possibilities, a sanctuary where nature's wonders unfold. By carefully designing, nurturing, and maintaining your garden, you can create a haven of beauty, tranquility, and connection. Embrace the joys and challenges of gardening, as you witness the growth of your plants, invite wildlife into your space, and savor the fruits of your labor. The outdoor garden is a testament to your love for nature and a place where you can find peace, inspiration, and a deep sense of fulfillment.

# Chapter 5: Hedges and Trees

Introduction: Hedges and trees play a vital role in the landscape, offering privacy, defining boundaries, and adding aesthetic appeal to outdoor spaces. They provide structure, shade, and a sense of permanence to gardens, parks, and public areas. In this chapter, we will explore the beauty and practicality of hedges and trees, their various types, their benefits, and how to care for them. Join us as we delve into the world of hedges and trees and discover how these remarkable plants can transform and enhance any outdoor setting.

Paragraph 1: The Importance of Hedges and Trees Hedges and trees are essential elements in landscaping, serving multiple functions. Hedges act as living fences, providing privacy, noise reduction, and wind protection. They also create boundaries and delineate different areas within a garden, adding structure and visual interest. Trees, on the other hand, offer shade, habitat for wildlife, and contribute to the overall ecosystem. They provide cooling effects, improve air quality, and add beauty and majesty to any landscape. The importance of hedges and trees cannot be overstated, as they create a harmonious and inviting outdoor environment.

Paragraph 2: Types of Hedges Hedges come in a variety of forms, each with its unique characteristics and benefits. Formal hedges, such as boxwood or yew, are meticulously pruned to create a precise and symmetrical shape. They are often used to create a sense of order and elegance in formal gardens. Informal hedges, on the other hand, have a more relaxed and natural appearance. Plants like privet, holly, or flowering shrubs can be used to create informal hedges, which provide a sense of privacy and attract wildlife with their flowers and berries. Evergreen hedges, such as cypress or laurel, offer year-round foliage and maintain their green color even during the winter months. Deciduous hedges, like beech or hornbeam, provide seasonal interest with their changing foliage colors.

Paragraph 3: Choosing the Right Hedge Selecting the appropriate hedge for your outdoor space requires careful consideration of various factors. Start by assessing the purpose of the hedge—is it primarily for privacy, noise reduction, or aesthetics? Consider the height and width requirements, as well as the growth rate of the chosen plant. Fast-growing hedges, such as Leyland cypress or bamboo, provide quick results but may require more frequent maintenance. Slower-growing options, like boxwood or yew, are more manageable but may take longer to achieve the desired effect. Soil conditions, sunlight exposure, and climate should also be taken into account to ensure the selected hedge thrives in your specific location.

Paragraph 4: Planting and Care of Hedges Proper planting and care are crucial to the success of hedges. Start by preparing the soil, removing weeds, and improving drainage if necessary. Dig a trench or individual holes for the hedge plants, ensuring they are spaced appropriately according to their mature size. Add organic matter to the soil to improve fertility and water retention. When planting, ensure the root ball is at the same level as the surrounding soil and backfill gently, firming the soil around the roots.

Regular watering is essential, especially during the establishment phase. Water deeply and consistently, allowing the soil to dry slightly between watering sessions to promote healthy root development. Apply mulch around the base of the hedge to conserve moisture, suppress weeds, and maintain a more stable soil temperature. Prune hedges regularly to maintain their desired shape and density. Timing and frequency of pruning will vary depending on the type of hedge, but generally, it's best to prune in early spring or late summer to encourage healthy growth.

Paragraph 5: The Beauty of Trees Trees are the anchors of any landscape, providing beauty, shade, and a sense of grandeur. They come in a wide variety of sizes, shapes, and colors, offering endless possibilities for creating a stunning outdoor environment. From towering deciduous trees with their vibrant foliage to evergreens that provide year-round interest, trees add depth, character, and a connection to nature in any setting.

Paragraph 6: Choosing the Right Trees When selecting trees for your landscape, consider the purpose and desired effect. Do you want shade, ornamental blooms, or attractive foliage? Assess the available space, taking into account the tree's mature height and spread. Consider the soil type, drainage, and sunlight conditions to ensure the chosen tree will thrive in your specific environment. Native trees are often a good choice, as they are well-adapted to the local climate and require less maintenance. Research the growth rate, disease resistance, and lifespan of the tree to make an informed decision.

Paragraph 7: Planting and Care of Trees Proper planting and care are essential for the long-term health and vitality of trees. Start by preparing the planting hole, ensuring it is wide and deep enough to accommodate the root ball. Remove any debris, rocks, or weeds from the hole. Gently place the tree in the hole, making sure it is positioned straight and at the appropriate depth. Backfill the hole with a mixture of soil and organic matter, gently firming it around the roots. Water the tree thoroughly after planting to settle the soil and provide initial hydration.

Regular watering is crucial during the tree's establishment period. Deep, infrequent watering promotes strong root growth. Consider installing a drip irrigation system or using a soaker hose to ensure water reaches the tree's root zone effectively. Apply a layer of mulch around the base of the tree, leaving a gap around the trunk to prevent moisture buildup and potential rot. Mulch helps retain soil moisture, suppress weeds, and regulate soil temperature. Fertilize the tree as needed, following the recommendations for the specific species and using a balanced, slow-release fertilizer.

Pruning is an important aspect of tree care. Remove any dead, damaged, or crossing branches to improve airflow and prevent disease. Prune in late winter or early spring when the tree is dormant to minimize stress and maximize regrowth. Consult a professional arborist for larger pruning tasks or if you are unsure about proper pruning techniques.

Paragraph 8: The Benefits of Hedges and Trees Hedges and trees offer numerous benefits beyond their visual appeal. They provide privacy, reducing noise pollution and creating a peaceful atmosphere. They act as windbreaks, helping to protect more delicate plants and outdoor living spaces from strong winds. Trees provide shade, reducing energy costs by cooling the surrounding area and creating a comfortable outdoor environment. They also improve air quality by filtering pollutants and releasing oxygen. Hedges and trees attract wildlife, providing habitat and food sources for birds, insects, and other creatures. They contribute to overall biodiversity and create a balanced ecosystem in your garden.

Conclusion: Hedges and trees are essential elements of any outdoor landscape, offering practical and aesthetic benefits. Hedges provide privacy, structure, and beauty, while trees add shade, majesty, and a connection to nature. By selecting the right plants, properly planting and caring for them, you can create a stunning and harmonious outdoor environment. Whether it's the neatly trimmed hedges or the towering trees with their vibrant foliage, these plants have the power to transform any space into a place of beauty and tranquility. Embrace the elegance and functionality of hedges and trees in your outdoor setting and enjoy the many rewards they bring.

# Chapter 6: The Vegetable Patch

Introduction:

The vegetable patch is a place of wonder and abundance, where the magic of nature unfolds before our eyes. It is a small corner of our world where we can connect with the earth, nurture life, and reap the rewards of our efforts. In this chapter, we will explore the enchanting realm of the vegetable patch, from the initial planning and preparation to the joys of planting, tending, and harvesting. Join us as we embark on a journey of discovery and learn how to create and cultivate a thriving vegetable patch.

Paragraph 1: Planning Your Vegetable Patch

Before putting shovel to soil, it is essential to plan your vegetable patch carefully. Consider the available space, sunlight exposure, and soil quality in your garden or yard. Choose a location that receives ample sunlight throughout the day, as most vegetables require at least six hours of direct sunlight. Assess the soil's fertility and drainage, and make any necessary amendments to improve its quality. Plan the layout of your patch, considering factors like crop rotation, companion planting, and the optimal spacing between plants. A well-thought-out plan will set the stage for a successful vegetable patch.

Paragraph 2: Soil Preparation

The quality of your soil is paramount to the health and productivity of your vegetable patch. Begin by clearing the area of any weeds, rocks, or debris. Loosen the soil using a garden fork or tiller, breaking up any compacted areas. Incorporate organic matter such as compost, well-rotted manure, or leaf mold to improve soil structure, fertility, and water retention. Test the soil's pH level and nutrient content and make necessary adjustments. Work the organic matter into the soil, ensuring it is evenly distributed and thoroughly mixed.

Paragraph 3: Selecting Vegetables for Your Patch

Choosing the right vegetables for your patch is a delightful task that requires careful consideration. Take into account your climate, available space, and personal preferences. Begin by selecting vegetables that thrive in your growing zone and have a high chance of success. Consider the size of your patch and choose a variety of vegetables that will provide a diverse and balanced harvest throughout the season. Include a mix of leafy greens, root vegetables, herbs, and fruiting crops. Research the specific growing requirements of each vegetable, such as soil pH, sunlight needs, and spacing, to ensure optimal growth and productivity.

Paragraph 4: Starting from Seeds

Starting your vegetables from seeds can be a rewarding and cost-effective way to populate your patch. Follow the instructions on the seed packets regarding planting depth, spacing, and germination requirements. Start seeds indoors in trays or pots, providing them with adequate light and warmth. Once the seedlings have developed a few sets of true leaves, gradually acclimate them to outdoor conditions before transplanting them into the patch. This gradual transition helps prevent transplant shock and ensures the success of your seedlings.

Paragraph 5: Transplanting Seedlings

Transplanting seedlings into your vegetable patch is an exciting step in the gardening process. Choose a cloudy or cool day to minimize stress on the young plants. Dig a hole slightly larger than the root ball of the seedling and gently place it in the hole, ensuring that the soil level matches the level of the seedling's stem. Firmly press the soil around the roots and water the newly transplanted seedlings. Provide them with shade or protection if the weather is particularly hot or windy. Monitor their progress closely and provide regular watering and care as they establish themselves in their new home.

Paragraph 6: Direct Sowing Seeds

Certain vegetables, such as carrots, radishes, and beans, are best sown directly into the soil in your vegetable patch. Prepare the soil by removing any weeds and creating a fine, crumbly texture. Follow the instructions on the seed packets regarding planting depth and spacing. Create furrows or holes in the soil, sow the seeds at the appropriate depth, and cover them gently with soil. Water the area thoroughly, keeping the soil consistently moist during the germination process. Thin the seedlings once they have grown a few inches tall, ensuring they have enough space to develop and thrive. Regularly monitor the moisture levels in the soil and provide water as needed to support the growth of your direct-sown vegetables.

Paragraph 7: Watering and Irrigation

Watering is a critical aspect of maintaining a healthy vegetable patch. Most vegetables require consistent moisture to grow and produce a bountiful harvest. Water deeply and evenly, ensuring the soil is adequately saturated. Avoid overwatering, as it can lead to waterlogged soil and root rot. Mulching around your plants with organic materials, such as straw or wood chips, can help retain moisture, suppress weed growth, and regulate soil temperature. Consider using drip irrigation or a soaker hose system to deliver water directly to the plant roots, minimizing water waste and promoting efficient hydration.

Paragraph 8: Pest and Disease Management

Keeping pests and diseases at bay is essential for the success of your vegetable patch. Monitor your plants regularly for signs of pests, such as aphids, caterpillars, or snails. Remove any pests you find by hand or use organic pest control methods like insecticidal soaps or natural predators. Implement companion planting techniques to deter pests, such as interplanting marigolds to repel nematodes or attracting beneficial insects like ladybugs. Additionally, practicing good garden hygiene by removing fallen leaves or damaged plant material can help prevent the spread of diseases. If necessary, use organic-approved fungicides or insecticides as a last resort.


Paragraph 9: Maintenance and Care

Ongoing maintenance and care are vital for the long-term health and productivity of your vegetable patch. Regularly weed your patch to eliminate competition for resources and prevent weed growth. Apply organic fertilizers, such as compost or well-balanced granular fertilizers, to provide essential nutrients to your plants. Monitor the growth of your vegetables and provide support, such as stakes or trellises, for climbing or vining plants. Prune or pinch back excessive foliage to promote air circulation and prevent overcrowding. Harvest your vegetables at their peak of ripeness for the freshest flavors and maximum nutritional value.

## Paragraph 10: Harvesting and Enjoying the Fruits of Your Labor

The joy of the vegetable patch culminates in the harvest, a time to reap the rewards of your hard work and dedication. Harvest your vegetables when they have reached the appropriate size and maturity. Use sharp garden shears or a knife to gently remove the produce from the plants, taking care not to damage the remaining foliage. Enjoy the flavors of your freshly harvested vegetables in salads, stir-fries, or simply as nutritious snacks. Share your abundance with friends and neighbors, and revel in the satisfaction of knowing that you have nourished both your body and soul with the fruits of your labor.

## Conclusion:

The vegetable patch is a source of endless wonder and delight, where the symphony of nature unfolds in vibrant colors and bountiful harvests. With careful planning, diligent care, and a touch of patience, you can create a thriving and abundant vegetable patch. Embrace the journey, savoring the moments of sowing seeds, tending to plants, and harvesting the fruits of your labor. Allow the vegetable patch to nourish not only your body but also your spirit as you connect with the earth and revel in the beauty of nature's cycles. So, roll up your sleeves, grab your gardening tools, and let the vegetable patch become your sanctuary of growth, nourishment, and joy.

# Chapter 7: The Herb Garden

Introduction:

The herb garden is a delightful and aromatic oasis that adds flavor, fragrance, and beauty to any space. Whether it's a small patch in your backyard, a collection of pots on a balcony, or a dedicated herb garden, cultivating herbs is a rewarding and fulfilling endeavor. In this chapter, we will explore the enchanting world of the herb garden, from selecting the right herbs to nurturing their growth and harnessing their incredible flavors and medicinal properties. Join us as we embark on a journey of discovery and learn how to create and maintain a thriving herb garden.

Paragraph 1: Choosing the Right Herbs

When planning your herb garden, consider the herbs that best suit your culinary preferences, gardening skills, and growing conditions. Popular culinary herbs like basil, rosemary, thyme, and parsley are versatile and can be used in a variety of dishes. Medicinal herbs like lavender, chamomile, and mint offer numerous health benefits and are a wonderful addition to any garden. Research the specific requirements of each herb, such as sunlight, soil type, and watering needs, to ensure their success in your garden.

Paragraph 2: Selecting a Suitable Location

Herbs generally thrive in sunny locations, receiving at least 6-8 hours of direct sunlight per day. Choose a well-drained area or consider growing herbs in containers or raised beds if your soil is heavy or poorly drained. Keep in mind that some herbs, like mint, can be aggressive spreaders, so consider planting them in containers to contain their growth. If space is limited, herbs can also be grown indoors on windowsills or under grow lights.

Paragraph 3: Preparing the Soil

Prepare the soil for your herb garden by removing any weeds, rocks, or debris. Herbs generally prefer well-draining soil with good fertility. If your soil is heavy or clay-like, amend it with organic matter such as compost, well-rotted manure, or peat moss to improve its texture and nutrient content. Work the organic matter into the soil to a depth of 6-8 inches, ensuring it is evenly distributed. Perform a soil test to determine the pH level and make necessary adjustments to create an ideal growing environment for your herbs.

Paragraph 4: Starting from Seeds

Starting herbs from seeds can be a cost-effective and rewarding way to begin your herb garden. Follow the instructions on the seed packets regarding planting depth, spacing, and germination requirements. Start the seeds indoors in trays or pots, providing them with adequate light and warmth. Once the seedlings have developed a few sets of true leaves, gradually acclimate them to outdoor conditions before transplanting them into your herb garden. This gradual transition helps prevent transplant shock and ensures the success of your seedlings.

Paragraph 5: Transplanting Seedlings

When transplanting your herb seedlings into the garden, choose a day with mild weather conditions. Dig a hole slightly larger than the root ball of the seedling and gently place it in the hole, making sure the soil level matches the level of the seedling's stem. Firmly press the soil around the roots and water the newly transplanted herbs. Provide them with shade or protection if the weather is particularly hot or windy. Monitor their progress closely and provide regular watering and care as they establish themselves in their new home.

Paragraph 6: Herb Garden Design and Layout

Consider the design and layout of your herb garden to create an aesthetically pleasing and functional space. Group herbs together based on their growing requirements and purposes. For example, culinary herbs can be grouped near the kitchen for easy access, while medicinal herbs can be clustered together for convenience. Use borders or pathways to define different areas within your herb garden and incorporate decorative elements such as garden ornaments or stepping stones to enhance its visual appeal. Consider the height and growth habits of the herbs when arranging them, placing taller herbs at the back and shorter ones in the front to create a visually appealing display. Additionally, interplanting herbs with flowers or companion plants can attract beneficial insects and add a splash of color to your garden.

Paragraph 7: Watering and Irrigation

Proper watering is crucial for the health and vitality of your herb garden. Most herbs prefer consistent moisture but are susceptible to root rot if overwatered. Water your herbs deeply, allowing the soil to dry slightly between waterings. Avoid watering the foliage, as this can promote fungal diseases. Consider installing a drip irrigation system or using a soaker hose to deliver water directly to the base of the plants, minimizing water waste and ensuring efficient hydration.

Paragraph 8: Pruning and Harvesting

Regular pruning and harvesting are essential for the continued growth and productivity of your herb garden. Prune your herbs to encourage bushier growth and prevent them from becoming leggy or woody. Remove any dead or diseased leaves or stems to maintain plant health. Harvest your herbs regularly, picking the leaves or stems as needed for culinary or medicinal purposes. Harvest in the morning when the essential oils in the herbs are at their peak. Regular harvesting will stimulate new growth and promote a continuous supply of fresh herbs.

Paragraph 9: Pest and Disease Management

Just like any garden, herbs can be vulnerable to pests and diseases. Monitor your plants regularly for signs of pests such as aphids, caterpillars, or mites. Use organic pest control methods like handpicking or spraying with a mixture of water and mild soap to deter pests. Companion planting with pest-repellent herbs like marigolds or planting herbs that attract beneficial insects can help keep pests at bay. Proper sanitation, such as removing fallen leaves or diseased plants, can prevent the spread of diseases. If necessary, use organic-approved fungicides or insecticides as a last resort.

Paragraph 10: Herb Preservation and Storage

Preserving the flavors and aromas of your herbs allows you to enjoy them even after the growing season has ended. Explore different methods of herb preservation, such as drying, freezing, or making herb-infused oils and vinegars. Harvest herbs in their prime, before they flower, for the best flavor and fragrance. Dry the herbs by hanging them upside down in a cool, well-ventilated area, or use a food dehydrator. Store dried herbs in airtight containers in a cool, dark place to maintain their potency. Freezing herbs in ice cube trays with water or oil is another convenient way to preserve their flavors.

Paragraph 11: Enjoying the Fruits of Your Herb Garden

The ultimate joy of an herb garden lies in the ability to savor the delightful flavors, aromas, and healing properties of fresh herbs. Incorporate your homegrown herbs into your culinary creations, adding a burst of freshness to salads, soups, sauces, and marinades. Experiment with herb combinations to create unique and delicious flavor profiles. Harness the healing powers of herbs by brewing herbal teas or creating homemade remedies and natural skincare products. Share the bounty of your herb garden with family, friends, and neighbors, spreading the love and appreciation for these incredible plants.

Conclusion:

The herb garden is a sanctuary of scents, flavors, and natural remedies, offering a multitude of benefits for both the palate and the body. Through careful selection, cultivation, and care, you can create a thriving herb garden that brings beauty, fragrance, and culinary delights to your life. Embrace the art of growing herbs, and let your garden become a haven of inspiration and wellness. Allow the enchanting aromas and vibrant colors to invigorate your senses as you explore the world of herbs. So, embark on this herbal journey, sowing the seeds of knowledge and nurturing the growth of your own herb garden. Discover the joy of cultivating herbs, from selecting the perfect varieties to harvesting and preserving their aromatic treasures. Whether you have a small balcony or a spacious backyard, the herb garden is a versatile and rewarding addition to any home.

In this chapter, we have explored the various aspects of creating and maintaining a thriving herb garden. We began by discussing the importance of selecting the right herbs based on your culinary preferences and growing conditions. We then delved into the process of choosing a suitable location and preparing the soil to provide an optimal environment for your herbs to thrive.

We explored different methods of starting your herb garden, including growing herbs from seeds and transplanting seedlings. Additionally, we discussed the importance of designing and arranging your herb garden to create a visually appealing and functional space. Proper watering and irrigation techniques were emphasized to ensure the health and vitality of your herbs.

We also addressed the importance of pruning and harvesting to encourage continuous growth and productivity. Managing pests and diseases through organic methods was discussed, highlighting the use of companion planting and good garden hygiene practices.

The chapter further explored the art of preserving herbs, allowing you to enjoy their flavors and aromas throughout the year. From drying and freezing to making herb-infused oils and vinegars, the possibilities are endless. Finally, we emphasized the joy of utilizing your homegrown herbs in culinary creations, herbal teas, remedies, and natural skincare products.

As you embark on your herb gardening journey, remember to embrace the beauty and versatility of herbs. Allow their scents to transport you to distant lands, their flavors to elevate your dishes, and their healing properties to nourish your body and mind. Discover the endless possibilities and explore the rich world of herbs, creating a garden that not only enhances your culinary experiences but also adds a touch of natural beauty and well-being to your life.

# **Chapter 8: Working in the Garden**

Introduction:

Working in the garden is a rewarding and fulfilling endeavor that connects us with nature, promotes physical activity, and allows us to witness the beauty of growth and transformation. Whether you have a small backyard plot, a community garden, or a vast expanse of land, tending to plants, sowing seeds, and nurturing the soil can bring immense joy and satisfaction. In this chapter, we will explore the various aspects of working in the garden, from preparing the soil to planting, maintaining, and harvesting your crops. Join us as we delve into the art and science of gardening and discover the many benefits it brings.

Paragraph 1: Assessing Your Garden Space

Before you embark on your gardening journey, it's important to assess your garden space. Consider the size, layout, and characteristics of your garden area. Take note of the amount of sunlight it receives throughout the day, as this will determine which plants will thrive in different areas. Additionally, assess the soil quality, drainage, and any existing structures or features that may impact your gardening plans.

## Paragraph 2: Planning Your Garden Layout

A well-planned garden layout is essential for maximizing space and ensuring a harmonious arrangement of plants. Sketch out your garden space, marking areas for different purposes such as vegetable beds, flower borders, or herb gardens. Consider the principles of companion planting to optimize plant health and deter pests. Plan for pathways, water sources, and potential support structures like trellises or stakes.

## Paragraph 3: Soil Preparation and Improvement

Preparing the soil is crucial for healthy plant growth. Begin by removing any weeds, rocks, or debris from the planting area. Test the soil pH and fertility levels to determine if any amendments are needed. Incorporate organic matter such as compost, well-rotted manure, or peat moss to improve soil structure, moisture retention, and nutrient content. Use a garden fork or tiller to loosen compacted soil, ensuring roots can penetrate easily.

## Paragraph 4: Selecting and Starting Seeds

Choosing high-quality seeds is vital for successful gardening. Consider factors such as plant variety, growth habit, disease resistance, and maturity time. Read seed packets or catalog descriptions to understand planting depth, spacing, and germination requirements. Start seeds indoors according to their specific requirements, providing adequate light, warmth, and moisture. Transplant seedlings outdoors when they have developed a few sets of true leaves and weather conditions are favorable.

Paragraph 5: Transplanting Seedlings and Direct Sowing

Transplant seedlings into the garden when they are strong and well-established. Dig holes slightly larger than the root ball, ensuring proper spacing between plants. Gently place the seedling in the hole and backfill with soil, firming it around the roots. Water thoroughly to help the seedling settle in its new environment. Alternatively, some plants can be directly sown into the garden, following spacing and depth guidelines on the seed packet.

Paragraph 6: Watering and Irrigation

Proper watering is crucial for plant health and productivity. Water your garden deeply and evenly, allowing the soil to dry slightly between waterings. Aim for morning or evening watering to minimize evaporation. Consider using a soaker hose or drip irrigation system to deliver water directly to the base of plants, reducing water waste and promoting deep root growth. Mulching around plants helps retain moisture and suppresses weed growth.

Paragraph 7: Garden Maintenance and Weed Control

Regular garden maintenance is essential to keep your plants healthy and productive. Monitor your garden for pests, diseases, and nutrient deficiencies. Remove weeds regularly to prevent competition for resources and minimize the risk of pests and diseases. Use organic mulch or weed barriers to suppress weed growth and retain moisture in the soil. Implement organic pest control methods such as handpicking, using insecticidal soaps, or introducing beneficial insects to keep pests in check.

Monitor plants for signs of disease and promptly address any issues with appropriate organic treatments. Additionally, provide support structures such as trellises or cages for climbing plants to ensure proper growth and prevent damage.

Paragraph 8: Pruning and Training Plants

Pruning plays a vital role in maintaining plant health, shape, and productivity. Regularly prune plants to remove dead or diseased branches, improve airflow, and stimulate new growth. Train climbing plants along supports to maximize space and promote better fruit production. Understand the pruning needs of different plant varieties and time your pruning activities accordingly to avoid interfering with flowering or fruiting.

Paragraph 9: Fertilizing and Nutrient Management

Proper fertilization is key to ensuring plants receive essential nutrients for optimal growth. Conduct soil tests to determine nutrient deficiencies and adjust fertilization accordingly. Use organic fertilizers, such as compost, well-rotted manure, or organic granular fertilizers, to provide a balanced nutrient supply. Apply fertilizers according to package instructions and avoid overuse, which can lead to nutrient imbalances or environmental pollution.

Paragraph 10: Harvesting and Enjoying the Fruits of Your Labor

The joy of gardening culminates in the harvest. Each plant has its unique harvesting requirements, and it's important to learn when and how to harvest different crops. Harvest vegetables when they are at their peak of ripeness and flavor. Use sharp, clean tools to prevent damage to plants and ensure a clean harvest. Enjoy the fruits of your labor by incorporating fresh produce into your meals, sharing with friends and neighbors, or preserving the abundance through canning, freezing, or drying.

Paragraph 11: Garden Pest and Disease Management

Garden pests and diseases can pose challenges to your plants. Regularly inspect your garden for signs of pests such as aphids, caterpillars, or snails. Implement integrated pest management techniques, such as handpicking, introducing beneficial insects, or using organic insecticides when necessary. Monitor plants for signs of diseases like powdery mildew or blight, and promptly take appropriate measures to minimize their spread, such as removing infected plants or applying organic disease control methods.

Paragraph 12: Reflection and Enjoyment

Working in the garden is not just about the physical labor; it's also a time for reflection and enjoyment. Take moments to appreciate the beauty of your garden, the fragrance of blooming flowers, and the satisfaction of nurturing life. Embrace the therapeutic benefits of gardening, which can reduce stress, improve mental well-being, and provide a sense of accomplishment. Share your garden experiences with others, join gardening communities, and continue to learn and grow as a gardener.

Conclusion:

Working in the garden is a labor of love that allows us to connect with nature, nurture life, and reap the rewards of our efforts. From preparing the soil to planting, maintaining, and harvesting, every step in the gardening process contributes to the growth and vitality of our plants. By following proper techniques, embracing organic practices, and staying attuned to the needs of our garden, we can create a thriving and bountiful outdoor space. So, roll up your sleeves, put on your gardening gloves, and embark on this journey of working in the garden. Enjoy the beauty, the flavors, and the sense of fulfillment that comes from cultivating your own little piece of nature.

# Chapter 8: Getting Rid of Garden Pests

Introduction:

Gardening is a fulfilling and rewarding endeavor, but it often comes with the challenge of dealing with garden pests. These unwelcome visitors can wreak havoc on our plants, causing damage, disease, and frustration. However, with proper knowledge and proactive measures, we can effectively manage and get rid of garden pests in an environmentally friendly manner. In this chapter, we will explore various strategies and techniques to combat garden pests and create a healthy, thriving garden ecosystem.

Paragraph 1: Understanding Garden Pests

Garden pests are a common challenge that gardeners face when nurturing their plants. These pests can range from insects and mites to snails, slugs, and even larger animals like rabbits and deer. Understanding the various types of pests and their behavior is essential in effectively managing and controlling their populations. Let's delve into the world of garden pests and gain a deeper understanding of their characteristics.

Insects are one of the most common types of garden pests. They come in various forms, including beetles, caterpillars, aphids, and whiteflies, to name a few. Insects can cause damage by feeding on plant foliage, flowers, fruits, or roots. Some insects also transmit diseases, further compromising plant health. Understanding the life cycles and feeding habits of specific insects can help identify and control them effectively.

Mites are another type of pest that can infest gardens. These tiny arachnids feed on plant sap, causing damage to leaves and stems. They are often difficult to spot due to their small size. Spider mites, for example, are known for their ability to reproduce rapidly and can quickly infest plants, particularly during hot and dry conditions. Regular monitoring and early detection are key to managing mite infestations.

Snails and slugs are common garden pests that feed on plant foliage, particularly in moist environments. Their feeding activity can lead to unsightly holes in leaves and the destruction of young seedlings. These pests are often more active at night, making them challenging to spot. Creating barriers or implementing organic pest control methods can help manage snail and slug populations effectively.

Larger animals like rabbits, deer, or rodents can also cause significant damage to gardens. They may feed on plants or dig up bulbs and tubers. Fencing, netting, or repellents are often used to protect gardens from these larger pests. Understanding their feeding patterns and behaviors can help develop appropriate strategies for deterrence and prevention.

Diseases caused by fungi, bacteria, or viruses can also affect plants in the garden. These diseases can lead to wilting, discoloration, or deformity of plant parts. Proper sanitation, good airflow, and regular inspection of plants can help prevent the spread and development of diseases. It is essential to promptly remove and dispose of infected plants to prevent further contamination.

To effectively manage garden pests, it is important to adopt an integrated pest management (IPM) approach. This approach combines preventive measures, cultural practices, and targeted interventions to minimize pest populations while minimizing harm to beneficial organisms and the environment. IPM strategies include practices such as crop rotation, companion planting, biological controls, and the judicious use of organic or chemical pesticides when necessary.

Understanding the life cycles, feeding habits, and behaviors of garden pests is crucial for developing effective pest management strategies. Regular monitoring, early detection, and prompt action are key to preventing pest outbreaks and minimizing damage. By implementing preventive measures and employing integrated pest management techniques, gardeners can strike a balance between maintaining plant health and managing pest populations.

In conclusion, garden pests come in various forms and can cause significant damage to plants if not properly managed. Understanding the characteristics and behaviors of pests is essential in developing effective control strategies. By adopting preventive measures, implementing integrated pest management techniques, and staying vigilant, gardeners can successfully navigate the challenges posed by garden pests and enjoy healthy and thriving gardens.

Paragraph 2: Prevention and Cultural Practices

The first line of defense against garden pests is prevention. Implementing good cultural practices can help create an environment that discourages pests from infesting your garden. This includes proper soil preparation, crop rotation, companion planting, and providing adequate plant spacing. Creating physical barriers, such as fences or netting, can also protect plants from larger pests.

Paragraph 3: Encouraging Beneficial Insects

When it comes to pest control in the garden, it's easy to focus solely on eradicating pests. However, a more sustainable and natural approach involves harnessing the power of beneficial insects. These helpful creatures act as natural predators, preying on garden pests and keeping their populations in check. By encouraging beneficial insects to thrive in your garden, you can create a balanced ecosystem that minimizes the need for chemical pesticides. Let's explore how you can attract and support beneficial insects in your garden.

One of the best ways to attract beneficial insects is to provide them with the resources they need to thrive. These resources include food, water, shelter, and a conducive environment. Planting a diverse array of flowering plants, especially those with small, nectar-rich flowers, can act as a valuable food source for beneficial insects. Examples include dill, fennel, yarrow, and cosmos. These plants not only provide nectar for adult insects but also attract prey species that serve as food for beneficial larvae.

Water sources are also important for beneficial insects. Providing shallow dishes filled with water or installing a small pond or water feature can create an oasis for beneficial insects to drink and reproduce. Remember to regularly clean and refresh the water to prevent the breeding of mosquitoes.

Shelter is crucial for beneficial insects to seek refuge and overwinter. Incorporating various plant structures such as dense shrubs, perennial grasses, and ground covers can provide hiding spots and protection from extreme weather conditions. Leaving some plant debris, like fallen leaves or dead stems, can also serve as nesting sites for beneficial insects.

Avoiding the use of broad-spectrum pesticides is essential for preserving beneficial insects. These chemicals can indiscriminately kill both pests and beneficial insects, disrupting the natural balance of your garden ecosystem. Instead, opt for targeted or organic pest control methods that specifically target pests while minimizing harm to beneficial insects.

Introducing beneficial insects to your garden can be a proactive approach to pest management. Ladybugs, lacewings, and praying mantises are well-known predators that can be purchased and released in your garden. These insects can quickly establish themselves and provide ongoing pest control. However, it's important to release them at the appropriate time and in suitable conditions to ensure their success.

Companion planting is another effective strategy to attract beneficial insects. Some plants release natural chemicals that repel pests or attract beneficial insects. For example, planting marigolds, nasturtiums, or petunias near vegetable crops can help repel aphids and attract beneficial insects like hoverflies and ladybugs.

Encouraging beneficial insects in your garden requires patience and observation. Regularly monitor your garden to identify beneficial insects and their activities. Learn to recognize their larvae, eggs, and feeding patterns. By familiarizing yourself with these beneficial species, you can take steps to protect them and create an environment that supports their population.

In conclusion, encouraging beneficial insects is a sustainable and natural way to manage garden pests. By providing food, water, shelter, and a pesticide-free environment, you can attract and support these helpful creatures. They will work diligently to control pest populations, reducing the need for chemical pesticides. Embrace the power of beneficial insects and create a thriving, balanced garden ecosystem that benefits both your plants and the environment.

Paragraph 4: Organic Pest Control Methods

Organic pest control methods focus on using natural substances and techniques to manage pests. This includes using insecticidal soaps, neem oil, horticultural oils, and homemade remedies like garlic or chili pepper sprays. These methods are safe for humans, beneficial insects, and the environment.

Paragraph 5: Companion Planting

Companion planting involves strategically planting certain plants together to enhance pest control. For example, planting marigolds near vegetables can repel nematodes, while planting herbs like basil or dill can deter aphids. Companion planting can also attract beneficial insects that prey on garden pests.

Paragraph 6: Mechanical Pest Control

Mechanical pest control involves physically removing or deterring pests from the garden. This can include handpicking larger insects like caterpillars or using traps for slugs and snails. Installing physical barriers like row covers or sticky traps can also prevent pests from reaching your plants.

Paragraph 7: Biological Controls

Biological controls involve introducing natural enemies of pests into the garden. This includes releasing beneficial insects like ladybugs or lacewings that feed on aphids, or using nematodes to control soil-dwelling pests. Biological controls are an effective and environmentally friendly way to manage pest populations.

Paragraph 8: Integrated Pest Management (IPM)

Integrated Pest Management combines various pest control methods to create a comprehensive and sustainable approach. IPM involves monitoring pest populations, identifying thresholds for intervention, and selecting the most appropriate control methods. It focuses on minimizing pesticide use and promoting long-term pest management solutions.


Paragraph 9: Using Traps and Barriers

Traps and barriers can be effective in capturing or excluding pests from specific areas. Sticky traps can be used to catch flying insects like whiteflies or fruit flies. Physical barriers like netting or fences can protect plants from larger pests such as deer or rabbits.


Paragraph 10: Cultural Control Techniques

Cultural control techniques involve modifying the garden environment to deter pests. This can include practicing good sanitation by removing plant debris, regularly inspecting plants for signs of infestation, and promptly removing and destroying affected plants. Proper watering and fertilization practices can also promote plant health and resilience, making them less susceptible to pests.


Paragraph 11: Natural Predators and Biological Controls

Harnessing the power of natural predators is an effective way to manage garden pests. Encouraging birds, bats, frogs, or beneficial insects like praying mantises and spiders can help control pest populations. Providing habitats such as birdhouses, bat boxes, or insect hotels can attract these natural predators to your garden.

Paragraph 12: Organic Pest Repellents

There are several organic pest repellents that can deter pests from your garden. For example, using garlic or onion sprays can repel pests like aphids and caterpillars. Planting aromatic herbs like rosemary, lavender, or mint can also help deter pests with their strong scents.

Paragraph 13: Crop Rotation

Crop rotation is a technique where different plant families are rotated in specific areas of the garden each year. This helps break the lifecycle of pests that target specific plant families. By rotating crops, pests that rely on a particular plant for survival will struggle to find their preferred host plants.

Paragraph 14: Monitoring and Early Intervention

Regular monitoring of your garden is crucial for early pest detection. Inspect plants for signs of damage, chewed leaves, or discolored foliage. Keep an eye out for pests or their eggs, and take action at the first sign of infestation. Early intervention can prevent pests from multiplying and causing widespread damage.

Paragraph 15: Consistency and Persistence

Consistency and persistence are two key qualities that play a significant role in achieving success in any endeavor, including gardening. When it comes to gardening, these qualities are particularly crucial in maintaining a thriving and flourishing garden. Consistency refers to the regularity and steadfastness in carrying out necessary tasks, while persistence is the determination to keep going despite challenges or setbacks. Let's explore why consistency and persistence are essential in gardening.

Consistency in gardening involves adhering to a routine and following through with necessary tasks. It means consistently watering plants, providing the appropriate amount of sunlight, and ensuring proper soil nutrition. Consistent care helps establish a healthy environment for plants, allowing them to grow and develop optimally. It also creates stability, reducing the risk of stress or shock that plants may experience due to inconsistent care. By consistently tending to your garden, you create a reliable and supportive environment for plant growth.

Moreover, consistency in gardening extends beyond basic care. It involves maintaining a regular schedule for tasks such as pruning, fertilizing, and pest control. By consistently performing these tasks, you can prevent problems before they arise or become severe. Regular pruning promotes healthier plant growth, while timely fertilization ensures plants receive the necessary nutrients for robust development. Consistency in pest control measures helps keep harmful insects or diseases at bay, protecting your plants from potential damage.

Persistence is equally vital in gardening. Gardening, like any other endeavor, presents challenges and obstacles. There may be times when plants fail to thrive, unexpected weather events occur, or pests invade your garden. In such situations, persistence becomes crucial. Instead of giving up, a persistent gardener continues to learn, adapt, and find solutions to overcome these challenges. They may research alternative methods, seek advice from experienced gardeners, or experiment with different approaches. This determination and perseverance allow them to navigate through setbacks and ultimately achieve success.

Persistence is particularly valuable when faced with setbacks or failures. A persistent gardener understands that gardening is a continuous learning process. They embrace failures as opportunities for growth and improvement, viewing them as valuable lessons rather than reasons to quit. They persistently seek solutions, making adjustments based on their observations and experiences. This resilience and adaptability enable them to overcome obstacles and ultimately achieve their gardening goals.

Consistency and persistence go hand in hand in gardening. Consistency provides the foundation for healthy plant growth, while persistence helps overcome challenges and setbacks. By consistently providing care, tending to tasks, and following a routine, you create a stable and nurturing environment for your plants. Meanwhile, persistence allows you to navigate through difficulties, learn from mistakes, and adapt your approach when necessary.

In conclusion, gardening requires both consistency and persistence. By consistently providing care, following through with tasks, and maintaining a routine, you establish a stable and nurturing environment for your plants. Additionally, persistence enables you to overcome challenges, learn from failures, and adapt your approach. Together, these qualities contribute to a successful and rewarding gardening experience. So, stay consistent in your care and remain persistent in the face of challenges, and you will reap the fruits of your labor in a flourishing and beautiful garden.

Conclusion:

Garden pests can be a persistent challenge, but with the right knowledge and proactive measures, you can effectively manage and eliminate them from your garden. By adopting preventive practices, encouraging beneficial insects, utilizing organic pest control methods, and implementing integrated pest management techniques, you can create a healthy and thriving garden ecosystem. Remember to stay attentive, monitor your plants regularly, and take prompt action when pests are detected. With perseverance and a balanced approach, you can enjoy a bountiful and pest-free garden that brings you joy and satisfaction year after year.

# Chapter 9: Garden tools

Introduction

Gardening is a wonderful hobby that allows us to connect with nature, nurture plants, and create beautiful outdoor spaces. To effectively maintain and cultivate a garden, having the right tools is essential. In this chapter, we will explore a comprehensive range of garden tools, their purposes, and how to use them effectively. Whether you're a novice or experienced gardener, understanding and utilizing the right tools will enhance your gardening experience and help you achieve the desired results. Let's dive into the world of garden tools and discover the essential equipment for every gardening enthusiast.

Shovels

Shovels are one of the most basic and versatile tools in a gardener's arsenal. They are designed for digging, lifting, and moving soil, compost, or other materials. A shovel typically consists of a long handle and a flat, slightly curved blade. There are different types of shovels, including round-point shovels, square-point shovels, and spades, each with its own specific uses.

Spades

Spades are similar to shovels but have a flatter blade and a shorter handle. They are commonly used for digging, edging, and cutting through tough soil or grass. Spades are particularly useful for creating clean garden borders, transplanting plants, and removing stubborn weeds.

Garden Forks

Garden forks, with their sturdy tines, are excellent tools for loosening compacted soil, turning compost, and lifting heavy clumps of earth. They are particularly effective in clay or heavy soil, as they help improve drainage and aeration. Garden forks come in different sizes and shapes, including digging forks and pitchforks, each serving specific purposes.

Rakes

Rakes are versatile tools used for various gardening tasks, including removing debris, leveling soil, and spreading mulch. They consist of a long handle and a series of teeth or tines. Leaf rakes, with their flexible tines, are ideal for gathering leaves and light debris, while garden rakes, with sturdy tines, are suitable for leveling soil, breaking up clumps, and removing stones.

Hand Trowels

Hand trowels are small, handheld tools with a narrow, pointed blade. They are indispensable for tasks such as planting, transplanting, and weeding. Hand trowels allow for precise digging in tight spaces, making them perfect for container gardening, flower beds, and small vegetable patches.

Pruners

Pruners, also known as secateurs, are essential for maintaining the health and appearance of plants. They are used for cutting and pruning branches, stems, and dead growth. There are two main types of pruners: bypass pruners, which have curved blades that pass by each other, and anvil pruners, which have a straight blade that cuts against a flat surface.

Loppers

Loppers are similar to pruners but have long handles for reaching higher branches. They are used for cutting thicker branches that are too large for pruners. Loppers provide the necessary leverage to make clean cuts and are available in various sizes and styles to accommodate different branch diameters.

Hedge Trimmers

Hedge trimmers are designed specifically for trimming and shaping hedges and shrubs. They come in manual and electric models, with electric trimmers offering increased power and convenience. Hedge trimmers have dual-action blades that oscillate back and forth, allowing for precise and efficient cutting.

Garden Shears

Garden shears, also known as hand shears or pruning shears, are versatile tools used for a variety of tasks, including cutting flowers, harvesting herbs, and shaping small plants. They have sharp blades with a scissor-like action, allowing for accurate cutting. Garden shears come in different sizes, with some models featuring serrated edges for cutting through tougher plant material.

## Garden Scissors

Garden scissors are smaller and more precise than garden shears. They are ideal for intricate tasks such as deadheading flowers, trimming delicate herbs, and harvesting fruits and vegetables. Garden scissors have sharp, fine blades that provide clean cuts without causing damage to surrounding plant tissue.

## Garden Knife

A garden knife is a versatile tool with a sharp, pointed blade. It is useful for a range of tasks, including cutting twine, dividing plants, and opening bags of soil or fertilizer. Some garden knives have serrated edges, making them suitable for sawing through tough plant material.

## Wheelbarrows

Wheelbarrows are essential for transporting heavy loads of soil, mulch, plants, and other garden materials. They consist of a shallow or deep tray mounted on one or two wheels, with handles for easy maneuverability. Wheelbarrows save time and effort by reducing the strain of carrying heavy items, making them indispensable in larger gardening projects.

## Garden Carts

Garden carts are similar to wheelbarrows but have a larger, more stable platform. They are ideal for hauling larger loads and can be pulled or pushed, depending on the design. Garden carts often come with added features such as removable sides or a dumping function, allowing for easy unloading of materials.

## Garden Hoses

Garden hoses provide a convenient and efficient way to water plants and clean outdoor spaces. They are available in various lengths and diameters, with options for different water pressure levels. Look for hoses made from durable materials that are resistant to kinking and twisting. Consider attachments such as nozzles or sprinklers for versatile watering options.

## Watering Cans

Watering cans are perfect for targeted watering, especially for delicate plants or areas with limited access. They come in various sizes and designs, with long spouts for precise pouring. Look for watering cans with removable rose attachments that provide a gentle shower-like flow, preventing soil erosion and damage to delicate foliage.

## Garden Sprayers

Garden sprayers are essential for applying fertilizers, insecticides, and fungicides to plants. They come in handheld or backpack designs, with adjustable nozzles for controlling spray patterns. Garden sprayers allow for even and accurate distribution of treatments, ensuring plant health and pest control.

Garden Gloves

Garden gloves protect your hands from cuts, blisters, and exposure to harsh chemicals. They come in various materials, such as leather or rubber, providing different levels of protection and dexterity. Choose gloves that fit well, allowing for comfortable movement and a good grip on tools.

Garden Apron

A garden apron is a practical accessory for keeping tools and small items within reach. It has multiple pockets and compartments to hold seeds, pruners, twine, and other essentials. A garden apron keeps your tools organized, saving time and preventing the loss of small items in the garden.

Garden Kneeler

Gardening often involves kneeling or squatting for extended periods, which can strain the knees and back. A garden kneeler provides cushioning and support, reducing discomfort and allowing for longer gardening sessions. Some garden kneelers can be flipped over to function as a bench, providing additional seating while working in the garden.

Garden Forks

Garden forks, also known as hand forks, are handy tools for loosening soil, removing weeds, and cultivating small areas. They have multiple curved tines that effectively break up compacted soil and loosen tangled roots. Garden forks are lightweight and easy to maneuver, making them ideal for working in raised beds or containers.

Seed Starting Trays

Seed starting trays are essential for starting seeds indoors before transplanting them into the garden. These trays have individual cells or compartments that hold the seeds and provide optimal conditions for germination. They often come with a transparent cover to create a greenhouse-like environment and promote healthy seedlings.

Garden Sprinklers

Garden sprinklers are useful for watering large areas of the garden efficiently. They come in various types, including oscillating, rotary, and pulsating sprinklers. Choose a sprinkler that covers the desired area and has adjustable settings for water flow and pattern. Sprinklers save time and ensure even watering across the garden.

Garden Ties and Supports

Garden ties and supports are essential for training and supporting plants as they grow. They include materials such as garden twine, plant ties, stakes, and trellises. Use them to secure plants to stakes or trellises, preventing them from bending or breaking under their weight. Garden ties and supports promote healthy plant growth and prevent damage caused by wind or heavy fruits.

Soil Testing Kits

Soil testing kits are valuable tools for understanding the nutrient content and pH level of your garden soil. They provide accurate measurements of essential elements such as nitrogen, phosphorus, and potassium. With the results, you can make informed decisions about soil amendments and fertilizer application to ensure optimal plant growth.

Garden Thermometer

A garden thermometer allows you to monitor the temperature of your garden soil and air. It helps determine the appropriate planting times for different crops and assists in identifying temperature extremes that may affect plant health. Some thermometers come with humidity gauges, providing a comprehensive view of the growing conditions in your garden.

Garden Pruning Saw

A garden pruning saw is a powerful tool used for cutting larger branches or tree limbs. It has a curved or straight blade with sharp, aggressive teeth that cut through wood efficiently. Pruning saws are essential for tree maintenance and can handle thicker branches that pruners or loppers cannot.

Soil Scoops and Spoons

Soil scoops and spoons are handy for transferring soil, potting mix, or compost from bags or containers into pots, trays, or garden beds. They have a deep, scoop-shaped design that allows for efficient and controlled soil movement. Soil scoops and spoons minimize mess and make filling containers or working with soil more manageable.

## Garden Edging Tools

Garden edging tools are used to create neat and defined borders between garden beds, pathways, and lawns. They can be manual tools like edging knives or electric tools like lawn edgers. Edging tools help maintain the shape of your garden and prevent grass or weeds from encroaching into unwanted areas.

## Garden Tool Storage

Proper storage of garden tools is essential for their longevity and easy access. Invest in a garden tool storage solution, such as a tool shed, wall-mounted hooks, or a tool rack. Keep your tools clean and dry to prevent rust and damage. Organized storage ensures that your tools are ready for use whenever you need them.

## Garden Tool Maintenance

Regular maintenance of garden tools is crucial for their optimal performance and longevity. Clean tools after use to remove dirt and debris, and sharpen blades regularly to ensure clean cuts. Check handles for wear and tear and replace them if necessary. Proper maintenance prolongs the lifespan of your tools and ensures they are always in excellent working condition.

Conclusion

Having the right garden tools is essential for successful gardening. The tools discussed in this chapter cover a wide range of tasks, from soil preparation and planting to maintenance and harvesting. By equipping yourself with the appropriate tools and understanding their uses, you can streamline your gardening tasks, increase efficiency, and achieve beautiful, thriving gardens. Remember to invest in quality tools, practice proper

# Chapter 10: Healthy Gardening

Introduction

Maintaining a healthy garden is not only about growing beautiful plants but also about fostering a sustainable and balanced ecosystem. Healthy gardening practices promote the well-being of plants, soil, wildlife, and humans. In this chapter, we will explore a range of strategies and techniques for creating and maintaining a healthy garden. From soil enrichment and water conservation to pest management and organic gardening, we will delve into the key principles and practices that contribute to a thriving and sustainable garden. Let's embark on a journey to discover the secrets of healthy gardening.

Understanding Soil Health

Healthy gardening starts with nurturing the soil. Soil provides essential nutrients, water, and support to plants. Conduct a soil test to determine its composition and pH level. Amend the soil with organic matter such as compost, manure, or leaf mulch to improve its structure, fertility, and water-holding capacity. Healthy soil promotes strong root development and enhances plant growth.

## Organic Gardening

Embracing organic gardening practices is a cornerstone of a healthy garden. Avoid using synthetic pesticides, herbicides, and fertilizers that can harm beneficial organisms and pollute the environment. Instead, opt for organic alternatives like neem oil, insecticidal soaps, and compost-based fertilizers. Organic gardening promotes biodiversity, safeguards human health, and protects the ecosystem.

## Water Conservation

Water is a precious resource, and conserving it is essential for sustainable gardening. Install a rainwater harvesting system to collect and store rainwater for irrigation. Use mulch around plants to minimize evaporation and maintain soil moisture. Employ drip irrigation systems to deliver water directly to plant roots, reducing water waste. Watering deeply but infrequently encourages deep root growth and conserves water.

## Companion Planting

Companion planting involves strategically placing plants that benefit each other in close proximity. Certain plant combinations can repel pests, attract beneficial insects, improve pollination, and enhance soil fertility. For example, planting marigolds near tomatoes can repel nematodes, while growing herbs like basil and rosemary alongside vegetables can deter pests.

## Crop Rotation

Rotating crops annually helps prevent soil depletion and the buildup of pests and diseases. Rotate crops within different plant families to minimize nutrient imbalances and reduce the risk of specific pests and diseases. For example, move tomatoes to a new location each year to prevent soilborne diseases such as verticillium wilt.

## Natural Pest Control

Incorporate natural pest control methods to manage garden pests without resorting to harmful chemicals. Encourage beneficial insects like ladybugs, lacewings, and parasitic wasps by planting nectar-rich flowers and providing suitable habitats. Use physical barriers like netting or row covers to protect plants from pests. Handpick pests like caterpillars or use organic insecticides as a last resort.

## Integrated Pest Management (IPM)

Implementing an integrated pest management approach combines various strategies to control pests effectively. IPM involves monitoring pest populations, identifying pest damage thresholds, employing cultural practices, utilizing biological controls, and using chemical controls only when necessary and least harmful to the environment. IPM promotes balance and minimizes the impact on beneficial insects and the ecosystem.

## Composting

Composting is an eco-friendly method of recycling organic waste into nutrient-rich soil amendment. Collect kitchen scraps, yard trimmings, and plant residues in a compost bin or pile. Turn the compost regularly to promote decomposition and aeration. The resulting compost enriches the soil with beneficial microorganisms, improves soil structure, and reduces the need for synthetic fertilizers.

## Beneficial Pollinators

Attracting pollinators such as bees, butterflies, and hummingbirds is crucial for a healthy garden. Plant a diverse selection of nectar and pollen-rich flowers that bloom throughout the growing season. These flowers include lavender, coneflowers, sunflowers, and bee balm. Provide water sources like shallow dishes with pebbles for butterflies and bees to drink from. Avoid using pesticides that can harm pollinators and their habitats.

## Weed Management

Controlling weeds is essential for maintaining the health and aesthetics of a garden. Regularly remove weeds by hand or with the help of gardening tools like hoes or cultivators. Apply mulch to suppress weed growth and conserve soil moisture. Avoid using chemical herbicides that can harm beneficial plants and contaminate the soil.

## Proper Plant Spacing

Proper plant spacing allows for adequate air circulation and sunlight penetration, reducing the risk of diseases and promoting healthy plant growth. Follow spacing guidelines provided on seed packets or plant tags. Overcrowding can lead to increased competition for nutrients and water, as well as the spread of diseases.

## Seasonal Planting

Planting vegetables, flowers, and herbs at the appropriate times ensures optimal growth and productivity. Consult a planting calendar specific to your region to determine the best times to sow seeds or transplant seedlings. Seasonal planting takes into account factors such as temperature, frost dates, and daylight hours, allowing plants to thrive in their preferred conditions.

## Mulching

Mulching is an effective technique for suppressing weeds, conserving moisture, moderating soil temperature, and enriching the soil. Apply a layer of organic mulch, such as wood chips, straw, or shredded leaves, around plants. Mulch also acts as a natural insulator during colder months, protecting plant roots from temperature fluctuations.

## Regular Maintenance

Regular garden maintenance plays a vital role in maintaining a healthy garden. Monitor plants for signs of pests, diseases, or nutrient deficiencies. Prune and remove dead or diseased plant parts to promote healthy growth. Remove spent flowers to encourage continuous blooming and prevent the plant from diverting energy into seed production.

## Continuous Learning

Gardening is a lifelong learning process, and staying informed about best practices and new techniques is key to maintaining a healthy garden. Join gardening communities, attend workshops, and read reputable gardening resources to expand your knowledge. Experiment with new methods and adapt your gardening practices based on your observations and experiences.

## Conclusion

A healthy garden is a reflection of a harmonious relationship between plants, soil, beneficial organisms, and gardeners. By implementing the principles of healthy gardening, such as soil enrichment, water conservation, natural pest control, and organic practices, you can create a thriving and sustainable garden. Embrace the joy of nurturing plants while respecting the environment and promoting the well-being of all living beings in your garden. Happy and healthy gardening!

# **Conclusion:**

Gardening is a transformative and fulfilling endeavor that allows us to connect with nature, nurture growth, and create beauty. Throughout this chapter, we have delved into various aspects of gardening, including soil health, plant care, pest management, and sustainable practices. By embracing the principles of healthy gardening, we can cultivate thriving and sustainable gardens that benefit both us and the environment.

Understanding the significance of soil health is fundamental to successful gardening. By nourishing the soil through the addition of organic matter, composting, and appropriate amendments, we provide plants with essential nutrients and create a fertile environment for their growth. Healthy soil promotes strong root development, vigorous plant growth, and improved overall plant health.

Implementing sustainable gardening practices is essential for minimizing our environmental impact and preserving natural resources. By conserving water through techniques such as drip irrigation, rainwater harvesting, and mulching, we can ensure efficient water usage and reduce water waste. Companion planting, crop rotation, and integrated pest management strategies help maintain a balanced ecosystem in the garden, minimizing the need for chemical interventions and promoting biodiversity.

Managing pests and diseases in a responsible and environmentally friendly manner is crucial for maintaining the health and vitality of our gardens. By utilizing natural pest control methods, attracting beneficial insects, and employing organic pest deterrents, we can effectively manage pest populations while minimizing harm to beneficial organisms and the wider environment. Regular monitoring and early detection of pest and disease issues enable us to take proactive measures and mitigate potential damage.

The selection and proper use of garden tools are vital for efficient and safe gardening practices. By utilizing the right tools for specific tasks, we can enhance our productivity, reduce physical strain, and achieve desired results. Regular maintenance and cleaning of tools ensure their longevity and optimal performance, making gardening tasks more enjoyable and effective.

Furthermore, gardening is an ever-evolving journey that offers countless opportunities for learning and personal growth. Staying informed about current trends, researching new techniques, and seeking guidance from fellow gardeners and experts enable us to expand our knowledge and refine our gardening practices. Continuous learning allows us to adapt to changing conditions, experiment with innovative approaches, and unlock the full potential of our gardens.

In conclusion, gardening is a deeply rewarding and enriching experience that encompasses much more than the act of planting and growing plants. It is a means of connecting with nature, nurturing life, and fostering a sense of responsibility for the environment. Through gardening, we cultivate a deep appreciation for the intricate web of life, recognizing the importance of preserving biodiversity and adopting sustainable practices.

May our gardens serve as vibrant and thriving oases of beauty, tranquility, and ecological balance. As we embark on our gardening journeys, let us cherish the connection we forge with the natural world, embrace the joy of nurturing living things, and celebrate the profound impact that gardening can have on our well-being and the health of our planet. Happy gardening!

Printed by Libri Plureos GmbH in Hamburg, Germany